Original title:
Beneath the Surface of a Smile

Copyright © 2024 Creative Arts Management OÜ
All rights reserved.

Author: Zachary Prescott
ISBN HARDBACK: 978-9916-90-574-6
ISBN PAPERBACK: 978-9916-90-575-3

Veils of Laughter

In the morning light, a chuckle blooms,
A dance of joy in sunlit rooms.
With every smile, a story spins,
Veils of laughter hide what begins.

Whispers float on gentle air,
Joyful moments, free from care.
Happy hearts weave threads so fine,
In a tapestry where sorrows align.

Laughter echoes, bright and clear,
Chasing shadows, drawing near.
In shared delight, our spirits soar,
Yet beneath, the silence roars.

A playful jest, a fleeting glance,
In revelry, we dare to dance.
But as the day fades into night,
The veils of laughter hide our plight.

Shadows at the Corners

In twilight's hush, shadows creep low,
Hidden whispers of pasts we know.
At corners where the daylight bends,
Silent stories, where night descends.

Figures linger, just out of sight,
Memories clash in the fading light.
Every glance a lingering doubt,
In the dark, what's left to scout?

With every step on gravel ground,
Echoes of footsteps softly found.
The air is thick with untold dreams,
In the shadows, nothing's as it seems.

They watch us from the edge of time,
Hints of hope in a darkened rhyme.
Yet in the blend of light and shade,
The truth of shadows, forever laid.

Echoes of Hidden Sorrow

In the silence, hearts might break,
Echoes of dreams that we forsake.
Lonely whispers in a crowded room,
Fading memories that twist and loom.

Behind each smile, a tale unfolds,
Silent battles, untold and bold.
Yet hope lingers like morning dew,
Catching light in shades of blue.

With every laugh, a tear is shed,
In joyous moments, pain can tread.
Yet through the fog, we find our way,
Seeking solace in another day.

Hidden sorrow is tightly bound,
A weight that often won't be found.
But in shared silence, hearts can heal,
Through echo's warmth, our truths reveal.

Whispers Behind a Grin

A fleeting grin hides tender pain,
In laughter's spell, we mask the rain.
With joyful eyes and fleeting cheer,
Yet whispers linger, sharp and clear.

Behind each smile, a tale is spun,
A delicate dance, a lost run.
The truth concealed, but close at hand,
In shadows where the heart must stand.

With every chuckle, the soul takes flight,
But deep within, there's hidden night.
Echoes of doubts in laughter's play,
Whispers speak of the trials we weigh.

Yet in connections, we find our grace,
In shared struggles, we dare to face.
Through every grin, the bond can grow,
For behind the joy, the truth will show.

The Cracks in Cheerfulness

Behind the smiles, the shadows creep,
Whispers of sorrow, buried deep,
Laughter dances on a fragile thread,
While tears of sorrow lie unsaid.

False brightness lights the heavy skies,
Yet underneath, the spirit sighs,
A mask of joy, a fragile guise,
Hiding truths that never rise.

Facades of Joy

Joy painted on with a hopeful brush,
Yet inside beats a heart in hush,
Colorful masks adorn the face,
Hiding the pain, a secret space.

In crowded rooms, we stand apart,
Sharing smiles while guarding hearts,
A grand illusion, bright and bold,
Yet stories of sorrow remain untold.

The Mask We Wear

We wear our masks, so bright and neat,
Each painted line conceals defeat,
In laughter's hold, we find our place,
Yet yearn for truth in open space.

The world expects a polished show,
While inside, the wild rivers flow,
In silence, we craft our charade,
Hiding the fear that life has made.

Gleaming Eyes

Eyes like stars, they shine so bright,
Holding secrets of the night,
In each glimmer, a story spins,
Of battles lost and silent wins.

Though faces beam, with joy displayed,
In those gleaming depths, fears invade,
A fleeting glance can so reveal,
The painful truth we mask and seal.

Clouded Hearts

Hearts once bright, now clouded gray,
Lost in thoughts that drift away,
The storms of life have left their mark,
Where there was fire, now lies dark.

Yet hope still flickers, faint and small,
A whispered promise through it all,
In tangled feelings, we find the way,
To break the clouds and greet the day.

Smiles that Hide

In a room filled with laughter,
Shadows linger, unseen.
Behind every bright grin,
Is a heart in between.

Masks worn with such grace,
Covering pain deep inside.
A façade of delight,
Where true feelings abide.

Every chuckle a sigh,
Every giggle a tear.
In the glow of the night,
Their true selves disappear.

Yet hope blooms like spring,
In the cracks of their smiles.
For the brave choose to feel,
The warmth that defiles.

The Dance of False Merriment

In the spotlight they twirl,
Chasing joy with a gleam.
Each step is a cover,
To mask what they deem.

With laughter that echoes,
As the music plays on,
They whirl in a frenzy,
Till the moment is gone.

Draped in illusions,
They sway with the night.
Hiding scars from the past,
In the soft, fading light.

Yet still, in the dark,
A glimmer remains bright.
A wish for the truth,
To conquer their fright.

Joy's Veil of Tears

A smile painted gently,
Like a soft morning sun.
Beneath the bright surface,
Lies a battle not won.

Each laugh is a whisper,
Of a sorrowful tale.
Contradictions abound,
In the storm that won't pale.

Joy wears a thin mask,
That often can break.
With the blink of an eye,
The facade starts to shake.

Yet finding such strength,
In the cracks of their heart,
They dance through the shadows,
With a brand new start.

The Fragile Art of Happiness

A smile like a petal,
Floating down with the breeze.
Delicate and fleeting,
It dances with ease.

In a world full of burdens,
Crafting joy takes a toll.
Balancing on a tightrope,
To keep their heart whole.

Each moment a treasure,
So easily lost,
They cradle their laughter,
And count every cost.

But within this fragility,
There's beauty to find.
In the cracks of their laughter,
Resilience is kind.

Radiance Wrapped in Shadow

In the quiet night, stars blink,
A dance of light on midnight's brink.
Secrets whispered in the dark,
Where shadows play, and dreams embark.

Moonbeams touch the silent ground,
In the stillness, echoes sound.
Light embraces every tear,
A paradox held close and dear.

Gentle winds weave through the trees,
A symphony that stirs the breeze.
Radiance falls, a soft caress,
While shadows cradle tenderness.

In this realm where contrasts thrive,
The heart's duality comes alive.
Finding peace in the unseen,
Beauty born from the in-between.

The Twisted Tales of Grin

In the corners of the fairground,
Dark secrets twist with laughter's sound.
A painted face hides tales untold,
As shadows dance, and truths unfold.

With every jest, a hidden sting,
A truth concealed in jesters' swing.
The laughter echoes, sharp and thin,
In every crack, the fears crawl in.

A crooked smile, a knowing glance,
In twisted words, the heart's dark dance.
We find our fears wrapped in the jest,
In Grin's embrace, we face the test.

Yet still, we laugh amidst the pain,
In every joy, a hint of strain.
For in these tales, we find a thread,
A twisted path where few have tread.

Joy in a Jester's Mask

Beneath the cap and bells, a soul,
A heart that strives to feel whole.
In laughter's guise, the truth concealed,
A world of pain, yet unappealed.

Each joke a whisper, soft yet loud,
In hidden sorrow, joy is proud.
With every fall and every rise,
The mask reveals both laughs and cries.

The juggling dreams, they dance and weave,
A fleeting moment, we believe.
In twirls of colors, time can bend,
Yet even jesters long for friends.

Behind the smiles, the heart still aches,
In the laughter, still the breaks.
For joy's a mask that one must wear,
A jester's plight, a cross to bear.

Submerged Sorrows of Laughter

In waves of chuckles, sorrows swell,
Drowning whispers no one can tell.
Beneath the surface, darkness lies,
As laughter masks the hidden cries.

Each giggle carried on the tide,
A fleeting joy, a broken pride.
We wear our smiles like gilded shells,
While deep inside, the silence dwells.

Yet in the jest, a spark can bloom,
A fleeting light amidst the gloom.
For every tear behind the grin,
A chance to breathe, a chance to win.

So let us laugh, though hearts may ache,
In every chuckle, hope we stake.
For sorrow's weight can often lift,
In laughter's arms, we find our gift.

The Burden of a Bright Countenance

A smile that shines like morning light,
  Hides shadows deep, a silent plight.
Beneath the glow, the heart does ache,
  For joy and sorrow's tangled break.

Each laugh a cover, a crafted mask,
  In perfect cheer, they often bask.
Yet in the night, the tears will flow,
  The burden of a bright show grows.

As dawn awakes, the truth will sway,
  Behind the bright, the soul's decay.
A tapestry of cheer and shame,
  The burden held in silence's name.

So let them smile, and let them weep,
  For joy's a secret, dark to keep.
Yet in the twilight, hope will sway,
  A balance struck in shades of gray.

Gleeful Facades and Hidden Pains

Wearing masks of joy each day,
Gleeful smiles lead hearts astray.
Behind the laughter, pain resides,
In shadows where the sadness hides.

For every cheer, a quiet tear,
The world can't see the hidden fear.
We dance along in bright attire,
Protecting hearts from false desire.

They twirl and spin in radiant light,
Yet within, there's an endless fight.
Complicated threads of bright and gray,
In gleeful facades, we lose our way.

Still, in the depths, a flicker glows,
A hope that only the brave know.
For with the sun, the shadows fade,
And hidden pains are slowly laid.

Joy's Subtle Layers

Joy softly wrapped in tender hues,
Layers dimmed by daily blues.
A fleeting glance, a hidden truth,
Unfolds the map of faded youth.

In laughter's echo, silence dwells,
Secrets lie, as laughter swells.
Each note of joy holds loss behind,
Memory's dance, both cruel and kind.

The sweetest moments often hide,
A bittersweetness deep inside.
For joy, like flowers, grows and fades,
In subtle layers, life cascades.

So cherish smiles, yet know the pain,
In every joy, a faint refrain.
For life blends hues in gentle streams,
A tapestry woven from our dreams.

The Art of Concealed Joy

In quiet corners, joy is spun,
A secret art, a hidden run.
With every step, a grace concealed,
The heart's true laughter is revealed.

We paint our days in vibrant shades,
While hidden joys slip through the blades.
The art of cheer, a delicate dance,
In shadows, lurks a fleeting chance.

Masked by time, concealed by choice,
The silent heart, it finds its voice.
In simple acts, true joy will play,
An artist's craft in soft array.

So let us cherish every spark,
The joy that flourishes from the dark.
For in the end, it's clear to see,
The art of concealed joy sets us free.

The Silent Symphony of a Smile

A smile dances soft and bright,
Whispers secrets in the night.
Each curve a note of sweet refrain,
A melody that soothes the pain.

In silence, joy begins to weave,
A tapestry that one can cleave.
Within the hearts, it lights the spark,
A symphony that sings in dark.

Through fleeting moments, grace unfolds,
In every glance, a story told.
The silent art we often miss,
A gentle touch, a fleeting bliss.

A smile can heal, can lift the weight,
Transform the cold and shift the fate.
In every face, there lies a tale,
The silent symphony prevails.

Ephemera of Joy

Joy flits like a butterfly,
A fleeting glimpse that passes by.
In laughter's echo, hearts take flight,
Moments shimmer, pure delight.

The fading light of day now wanes,
Yet joy remains despite the pains.
In every smile a world resides,
A fragile dance that never hides.

Leaves of laughter twist and twirl,
In gentle breezes, joys unfurl.
Though brief, their colors brightly shine,
Ephemera rich, a treasured line.

We grasp at dusk, the shifting light,
Chasing shadows with all our might.
Yet in these sparks, we find a way,
To hold the joy of yesterday.

The Dichotomy of Glee and Grief

Glee bursts forth in vibrant waves,
While grief quietly digs its graves.
Two tides that crash upon the shore,
A bittersweet dance forevermore.

In laughter's peak, a shadow looms,
The heart's bright blooms hide secret tombs.
Yet in this clash, we find the thread,
Of life's sweet songs, where love has bled.

Each joy that rises has its cost,
Yet every gain can feel like loss.
In tender moments, both can thrive,
A paradox where we survive.

We navigate these shifting sands,
With fragile hopes in trembling hands.
In every tear, a glimmer gleans,
The dichotomy of all our dreams.

Tapestry of Hidden Smiles

In shadows cast, the smiles reside,
A tapestry where we confide.
Threads of laughter, pain interlaced,
In quiet hearts, joy is embraced.

A knowing glance, a subtle cue,
Beneath the surface, feelings brew.
The hidden smiles that softly glow,
Reveal the truths we seldom show.

Woven tales and unsung songs,
In every heart, where hope belongs.
A patchwork bright of sorrow's hue,
A blend of life, both old and new.

This fabric thick with wishful dreams,
Holds fragments lost in whispered themes.
Within each stitch, there lies the spark,
A tapestry that lights the dark.

Masks of Mirth

Behind each mask we wear, a tale is spun,
In laughter's echo, we think we've won.
Yet shadows linger, deep and bold,
Hiding stories that are left untold.

The jester's grin, a fleeting guise,
Beneath it lies a heart that cries.
In revelry's light, we dance and sway,
But truth remains just a breath away.

When night descends, the masks fall low,
Revealing the scars we dare not show.
In every chuckle, a bittersweet sigh,
For the joy we share is bound to fly.

Yet still we play, in this grand charade,
For a moment's joy, the price is paid.
In masks of mirth, we seek the light,
Hoping to find our way in the night.

The Unseen Weight of Joy

Joy dances lightly, a feather's grace,
Yet beneath that thrill, there lies a space.
Where laughter bubbles, shadows creep,
A truth too heavy, too hard to keep.

The smiles we wear are tightly sewn,
In their bright fabric, a sorrow's grown.
For every moment of pure delight,
There's an unseen burden, hidden from sight.

With every cheer, a whisper calls,
Of dreams deferred and silent falls.
In every sparkle, a drop of dew,
Reflects the weight, it once just knew.

Yet still we grasp for joy's sweet thread,
Even as the heart feels heavy instead.
In tangled moments, we learn to cope,
Finding warmth in the shimmer of hope.

In the Stillness of Laughter

In laughter's stillness, a silence lies,
Echoes of joy, like whispered ties.
Moments captured, both fleeting and vast,
Unsung melodies from the past.

The heart beats soft, a gentle thrum,
In the pause between, a feeling's slum.
As laughter fades, a truth is found,
In the quiet space, our souls are bound.

Every chuckle holds a memory dear,
Tracing the paths that brought us here.
Though joy may wane, one truth stays bright,
In stillness, laughter gives us light.

So let us treasure the echoes we share,
In the quiet lull, love fills the air.
For in laughter's stillness, we come alive,
Awakening dreams that help us thrive.

Threads of Grief in a Festive Weave

In the tapestry bright, grief threads through,
Woven in joy, a bittersweet hue.
The festive cheer, a cloak we don,
Yet shadows whisper, we carry on.

Each celebration aches with love lost,
In the lights' glow, we count the cost.
With every smile, a tear may flow,
In the dance of joy, our hearts still know.

The music plays, and we move as one,
Yet haunted echoes of voices gone.
We raise our cups, in toast to the night,
For within the joy, there's room for plight.

So let the music play, let laughter ring,
For in our hearts, their love still sings.
In threads of grief, we find our peace,
In festive weaves, our joys don't cease.

The Hidden Tears in a Joyful Tune

In shadows cast by laughter's glow,
A fragile heart begins to know.
Beneath the smiles, a silent plea,
The hidden tears in joy set free.

With every note, a longing sigh,
A dance of joy, a bittersweet cry.
As music plays, the soul is bare,
In joyful tunes, we find despair.

Yet through the tears, the laughter flows,
A melody from which love grows.
For in the mix of joy and pain,
The music plays, again, again.

So let us sing in unison bright,
Embrace the sorrow wrapped in light.
For hidden tears do not define,
The joyful tune, the heart's design.

Hidden Echoes of a Grin

A smile so bright, yet eyes betray,
The echoes of what words can't say.
In silent moments, shadows creep,
Hidden echoes of the heart, we keep.

Behind the curve of every lip,
A memory clings, a fragile grip.
With laughter loud, the truths unwind,
In the soft hush, solace we find.

For in the jest, a depth concealed,
The laughter soft, the pain revealed.
Each grin a veil, a craft so fine,
Hidden echoes of a life entwined.

Let every chuckle glimpse the past,
In joyous notes, our shadows cast.
Embrace the light, the joy within,
Uncovering all the hidden grin.

The Veil of Laughter

Behind the mask of cheerful glee,
A world of thoughts, of what could be.
The veil of laughter softly hides,
A heart that aches, yet still abides.

In merry tunes, the truths collide,
With every jest, the tears confide.
Through joyous cries, the sorrow brews,
The veil of laughter only confuses.

A moment's fun, then silence reigns,
A fleeting joy, yet lingered pains.
The laughter echoes, shadows play,
As we stand masked in bright array.

So let us lift the veil and see,
The laughter's gift, the heart's decree.
In every chuckle lies the tale,
That life is more than just the veil.

Whispers Behind the Cheer

Amidst the laughter, soft and low,
Whispers of doubt begin to grow.
Behind the cheer, a tale untold,
The warmth of smiles, the hearts of gold.

With every chuckle, stories hide,
In the silence, feelings abide.
A fleeting joy, a glimpse of fear,
Whispers linger when none are near.

In the spotlight's glow, we stand so bold,
Yet shadows encircle, stories unfold.
The laughter dances, but cannot quell,
The whispers echo, a silent spell.

So let us cherish every tear,
Behind the smiles that we hold dear.
For in each giggle's gentle sway,
The whispers guide us on our way.

The Gravity Behind the Grin

In shadows lurk a tender tease,
A smile that hides beneath the breeze.
Bright laughter echoes, yet it bends,
For joy and sorrow often blend.

The heart may dance though eyes may weep,
Secrets buried, promises kept.
A surface gleams, but depths do know,
The weight of feelings planted low.

With every chuckle, there's a weight,
A push and pull within our fate.
In moments flaring, darkness fades,
Yet fears may linger in the shades.

And still we wear this playful guise,
As gravity tugs at hidden sighs.
Behind the grin, a story's spun,
Of battles lost and triumphs won.

Eclipsed Mirth

A joyous spark devoid of light,
Where smiles beguile the endless night.
In laughter's wake, the shadows creep,
As silence wraps the heart in deep.

Beneath the mask of cheerful flare,
Exist the whispers, burdens rare.
Each joyful joke a thin disguise,
For sorrow lingers in the eyes.

The stars may shine but clouds obtain,
A lingering pulse of writhing pain.
Amidst the joy, a void we sense,
Eclipsed mirth, our recompense.

So let the laughter swell and rise,
But know the truth that often lies.
Within the gleam, the heart does sigh,
A bittersweet cloud in the sky.

Unseen Currents of Gaiety

In rivers deep, like laughter flows,
A current hides where nobody knows.
The tide of joy, a silent song,
Yet underneath, we feel what's wrong.

With every chuckle, shadows play,
The light it gives, a fleeting ray.
For in the waves, the echoes dart,
Unseen currents pull at the heart.

The dance of glee with rhythms strange,
An intricate weave, a hidden change.
Bright smiles atop a restless sea,
A joyous mask, but not quite free.

Through whispered winds, the tales unwind,
In joyful laughter, we must find.
The unseen touch of gaiety's hand,
May guide us gently through the land.

Joy that Masks

A radiant face, a bright façade,
Hiding whispers of life's charade.
In every giggle, truth concealed,
A heart thus armored, fate unsealed.

Behind the laughter, silence reigns,
In hollow echoes, joy's disdain.
A mask of bliss, a polished sheen,
Yet shadows whisper where we've been.

The gleaming smile, a crafted jest,
To shield the heart from heaven's test.
When joy is worn as a sacred cloak,
True feelings smolder, scarcely spoke.

Yet still we dance, the masks we wear,
In vibrant hues, we seem to care.
For joy that blinds can oft protect,
But hides the shadowed intellect.

Facades of Delight

In gardens bright with painted flowers,
We wear the masks of joyful hours.
Their colors shine, a vivid show,
Yet in the shade, still whispers flow.

Beneath the laughter, secrets hum,
The heart confused, a steady drum.
Each smile a fine, deceptive art,
A game we play to hide the heart.

The sun sets low, the shadows creep,
A truth concealed, a silence deep.
We dance along this fragile line,
Where joy and sorrow intertwine.

In colors bright, in shadows cast,
We weave a world from broken past.
Yet in this space where dreams ignite,
We find our peace in fleeting light.

Mirrors of a Faintly Smiling Heart

In mirrors clear, reflections tease,
A faintly smile, a subtle breeze.
Behind the glass, a whisper sighs,
The heart's soft truth in masked disguise.

With every glance, a story told,
Of dreams once bright, now dimmed and cold.
Yet in the depths, a glimmer glows,
A warmth that only the heart knows.

Each joyful look, a silent plea,
For what is lost, for what could be.
In every laugh, a muted cry,
A fragile truth that lingers nigh.

And in the stillness, echoes call,
Reminders of both rise and fall.
With every shard, the heart embraces,
The beauty found in hidden places.

The Dance of a Concealed Spirit

In twilight's hue, the spirit sways,
A dance that masks the hidden ways.
With every step, a story flows,
A rhythm known, yet seldom shows.

Around the fire, shadows prance,
In silence, souls begin to dance.
Each movement veils an inner fight,
A spark concealed beneath the light.

With whispered songs, the night unfolds,
The heart's deep secrets, soft but bold.
In every twirl, a chance is spun,
The dance of two, yet both are one.

And when the moon begins to wane,
The spirit sighs, a sweet refrain.
In every pause, in every beat,
Lives a tale bittersweet and fleet.

Laughter as a Cover

In laughter's cloak, we hide our fears,
A veil of joy, a shield from tears.
With every chuckle, shadows fade,
Yet underneath, the heart is swayed.

Around us, mirth, a fleeting sense,
A cover soft, a pretense, dense.
Each joke a mask, a fleeting spark,
That lights the night, yet leaves a mark.

Through crowded rooms, we laugh aloud,
Yet in our hearts, a lingering cloud.
We chase the echoes, bright and clear,
But in the silence, truth draws near.

So let us laugh, but dare to see,
The layers deep, the heart's decree.
In laughter's arms, a truth uncovers,
The hidden pain that love discovers.

The Unveiled Grin

A flash of light, a spark so brief,
Unraveled truth behind the thief.
In smiles we find a gentle guise,
Where secrets dance beneath the skies.

In shadows cast by morning's glow,
The laughter hides what few may know.
A grin so wide, yet veiled in thought,
Reveals the battles bravely fought.

Behind each chuckle lies a tale,
Of whispered dreams that sometimes fail.
Yet in that fleeting, joyful glance,
We weave the threads of life's great dance.

With every smile, a hint of pain,
Wrapped tight in joy, a sweet refrain.
The unveiled grin holds life's embrace,
A hidden love, a fragile grace.

Undercurrents of Joyful Facades

Bright banners wave on streets of cheer,
While currents pull on hearts drawn near.
Playful masks, we wear with pride,
Yet underneath, the tides collide.

A laugh erupts, a joyous sound,
But depths of sorrow can be found.
In every cheer, a whispered sigh,
The hidden truths that underlie.

Festivals of laughter, bright and bold,
With stories waiting to be told.
Behind the scenes, the tears may flow,
While joy constructs its wondrous show.

Dance in motion, yet hold your breath,
For every smile may flirt with death.
In joyful facades, we wear our chains,
Undercurrents run through our refrains.

The Veiled Ascent of Laughter

Beneath the sun, the laughter rings,
A soft ascent on breezy wings.
Yet darkened notes weave through the song,
As echoes hum where hearts belong.

With every giggle, whispers glow,
The hidden depths we seldom show.
For joy can lift, yet weigh the soul,
In veiled ascent, a fractured whole.

Euphoria dances, moments fleet,
In laughter's grasp, we find retreat.
Yet shadows loom where bright eyes stare,
The veils conceal the weight we bear.

Yet through the masks, a light will shine,
In laughter's arms, we intertwine.
A path of joy, though fraught with strife,
In veiled ascent, we find our life.

The Hidden Weight of Happiness

A cheerful smile brightens the day,
Yet underneath, the heart may sway.
What glimmers gold may rust with time,
The hidden weight, a silent crime.

In joyous moments, shadows creep,
As laughter calls, the burdens seep.
For happiness can wear a mask,
Revealing not what hearts may ask.

Each joyous leap feels light as air,
Yet grounded low, there's weight to bear.
A smiling face hides tales unheard,
In happiness, a weight inferred.

Yet still we search for rays of light,
To counterbalance, take our flight.
In hidden weight, we find our strength,
For happiness can stretch great lengths.

Laughter's Silent Song

Whispers dance upon the air,
Joyful echoes everywhere.
Moments trapped in fleeting play,
Softly fading, gone away.

Glimmers shine in every eye,
Threads of glee that flit and fly.
With each smile, a story grows,
In silence, laughter's spirit glows.

Caught in warmth of tender cheer,
Every heartbeat draws us near.
Imagine joy that can't be sold,
A silent song, forever told.

The Mask of Happiness

Behind the smile, a tale concealed,
Emotions masked and hearts appealed.
Behind each grin, a hidden scar,
Bright faces often hide bizarre.

A painted face in crowded halls,
Laughter echoed, yet it calls.
In shadows, dreams may drift away,
Where true feelings often sway.

A moment's bliss, a fleeting glance,
Life's cruel waltz, a twisted dance.
Yet hope remains through every crack,
For joy's true light will find its track.

In the Depths of Delight

Beneath the waves of laughter's tide,
In sunlit pleasure, dreams collide.
Rippling moments swell and rise,
In the depths, true joy lies.

Together we dive, hearts unbound,
Within our souls, pure bliss is found.
Sinking softly, embracing the flow,
In these depths, we truly grow.

Glowing warmth from shared embrace,
In friendship's light, we find our place.
Through tempests tossed and trials faced,
Delight remains, ever graced.

Unspoken Tales of Grinning Faces

Silent nods and knowing winks,
In crowded rooms, a spirit links.
With every gaze, a story's spun,
Unspoken tales, two hearts as one.

In laughter's cradle, secrets bloom,
Fingers brush, dispelling gloom.
A glance exchanged, a smile unveiled,
In harmony, our spirits sailed.

Bound in friendship, time stands still,
Moments shared, a binding thrill.
In every grin, a world exists,
Unheard tales, forever kissed.

Unspoken Tales of the Heart

In whispers soft, the heart does speak,
Its secrets held, too shy, too weak.
Beneath the smiles, a storm may brew,
Unseen battles fought, yet few ever knew.

A glance can tell what words can't say,
In fleeting moments, hopes decay.
Yet in the silence, love survives,
A thread of light, where longing thrives.

Each beat a story, untold, unheard,
In quiet chambers, dreams deferred.
A language pure, devoid of sound,
In every ache, the truth is found.

So listen close when hearts collide,
In unspoken tales, our souls confide.
Embrace the quiet, let it unfold,
For in the silence, love is bold.

The Illusion of Delight

A painted smile, a cheerful guise,
The laughter dances, hides the cries.
In colors bright, we dress the pain,
An artful mask, a sweet refrain.

Behind the façade, shadows creep,
In empty laughs, sorrow deep.
The mirage glimmers, yet it fades,
In fleeting joy, our heart betrays.

We chase the light, avoid the gloom,
Yet darkness looms within the room.
The paradox of joy and strife,
An endless search for joyful life.

In every moment, we pretend,
But truth hides close, around the bend.
To seek the depth, embrace the night,
In shadows' grasp, we find our light.

Happy Faces, Heavy Hearts

They wear their smiles, a brilliant show,
Yet deep within, the sorrows grow.
Laughter rings, but eyes reveal,
The heavy hearts that never heal.

In crowded rooms, they play their part,
But loneliness clings to every heart.
The joy they share, a thin veneer,
A mask that hides their quiet fear.

Each face a story, layered and torn,
In silence forged, their spirits worn.
To look beyond the cheerful face,
Is to find truth in the hidden space.

Though they may laugh, and dance with grace,
The shadows linger, a tight embrace.
For happy faces may charm the eye,
But heavy hearts are where dreams die.

Beneath the Bright Exterior

Beneath the surface, storms may rage,
A brightly painted, fragile page.
With sunshine smiles, we cast a spell,
Yet deep within, we know too well.

A vibrant world, yet threads unwind,
In every laugh, a tear confined.
The tales unwritten, the truths we hide,
In hollow joy, the heart's confide.

The glimmering light, a deceptive glow,
Hides the echoes of silent woe.
For underneath, the stories flow,
In shadows' dance, the heartbeats grow.

With every flicker of the light,
We yearn for peace, we seek the fight.
To love the depths, embrace the fear,
Beneath the bright, the soul draws near.

Shadows of a Radiant Facade

Beneath the glow of painted smiles,
Lurk whispers soft, concealed in styles.
A laughter bright, yet tears lie still,
Behind the charm, a silent will.

Bright colors mask the fading light,
Where hopes once soared, they now take flight.
In every beam, a shadow's dance,
A careful move, a fleeting chance.

As hearts will yearn for truth's embrace,
They hide away, a secret place.
Masks we wear can weigh us down,
Yet some still sparkle, laugh, and drown.

Smiles in Disguise

Each smile wrapped in mystery's thread,
Hides all the words that go unsaid.
A playful glance can cloak the pain,
As joy and sorrow intertwine again.

In crowded rooms, the winks deceive,
While hollow laughs beg us believe.
For in the depth of each bright eye,
Lies tales of love and dreams that fly.

A joyous mask, so sweet to wear,
But truth can linger in the air.
With every chuckle, echoes creep,
In hearts that ache, and eyes that weep.

The Facade of Joy

Joy dances on the edge of night,
With laughter's tune, it takes to flight.
Yet under bliss, the shadows cling,
A careful act, the heart will sing.

Through painted lips and sparkling eyes,
The essence of the truth belies.
For every cheer, a hidden sigh,
In vibrant hues, a whispered cry.

Behind the scenes, the story weaves,
A tapestry of hopes and leaves.
In masquerades of cheer and play,
The facade holds the night at bay.

Secrets Behind Gleaming Eyes

In every glance, a story slept,
A world of secrets, long adept.
The shining surface softly glows,
Yet deep within, the silence grows.

Behind each twinkle, shadows lie,
With whispered fears that crawl and sigh.
For every spark that lights the dark,
Is just a cover, a longing mark.

The eyes may gleam with unwritten tales,
In hushed tones speak where silence prevails.
For hidden truths, they brave the skies,
And dance with all those gleaming eyes.

The Marvel of a Masked Heart

In shadows deep, the silence grows,
A hidden beat, where no one knows.
Behind the veil, a love profound,
A beating heart, without a sound.

The mask I wear, it glimmers bright,
Yet hides the truth, both day and night.
In gentle sighs, and whispered dreams,
A tale unfolds, or so it seems.

With every glance, a secret shared,
A fragile bond, the heart declared.
In laughter's glow, the world will see,
The marvel held inside of me.

So let the night embrace the spark,
A journey sourced from light and dark.
For deep within this masked delight,
A heart beats on, embracing light.

Masks of Merriment

Laughter rings, a joyful cheer,
With masks we dance, the world is near.
In vivid hues, our spirits soar,
As we explore the dreams in store.

Each face adorned, a playful guise,
In merriment, we find our prize.
With every twirl, the laughter flows,
From carefree hearts, the bliss only grows.

In masquerades of endless fun,
We cherish moments, one by one.
Beneath the masks, we are the same,
In unity, we share the game.

So raise a toast to joy and grace,
With masks of merriment, we embrace.
With every smile, a memory is spun,
In this grand tale, our hearts are one.

Laughter's Delicate Deceit

Chuckle softly, beneath the guise,
Where truth and jest wear false replies.
In playful tones, we find our bliss,
But hidden lies, we dare not miss.

A wink exchanged, a glance askew,
In laughter's web, the doubts ensue.
With every jest, the layers peel,
Revealing hearts, that yearn to heal.

Yet in this dance of foolish grace,
We find ourselves, in life's embrace.
Through laughter's lens, we see the light,
And bask in warmth, despite the fright.

So let us laugh and let us play,
In laughter's trap, we find our way.
For in deceit, a truth will grow,
A tender heart, that winds will blow.

Unicorns in the Gloom

In shadows cast, where fantasies lie,
Unicorns roam, beneath the sky.
With horns of light, they pierce the night,
A fleeting hope, a distant sight.

Through tangled woods, and whispers low,
The magic stirs, begins to glow.
In twilight's embrace, they dance and weave,
A secret world, we yearn to believe.

Yet gloom surrounds, a heavy veil,
As dreams collide, and shadows trail.
But in the dark, their spirits rise,
With every heart, that dares to try.

So seek the light, beyond the mist,
In unicorns, we find our tryst.
For even in gloom, if hearts are true,
The magic lives, to guide us through.

The Depth of a Simple Grin

A simple grin can light the night,
With warmth that banishes the fright.
It whispers tales of joy and grace,
Transforming hearts with soft embrace.

In stillness speaks a thousand words,
A quiet language, softly stirred.
Like sunbeams cutting through the gray,
It paints the world in brighter ways.

Each curve a story, sweet and small,
A bridge connecting one and all.
With just a nod, it gently weaves,
The fabric of what love believes.

In every grin, life's depths unfold,
A treasure trove of warmth to hold.
So simple yet profound, it seems,
A smile's the keeper of our dreams.

Joy's Fragile Armor

Joy, a fragile shine we wear,
An armor light, a vibrant flare.
It shields the heart from scorn and blight,
A burst of color in the night.

But tender is this gleaming shell,
It bends and breaks, it swells and swells.
A fleeting spark, yet brightly bold,
A dance of warmth in stories told.

Behind the laughter, tears may hide,
Yet joy will always seek to guide.
Through every storm, it finds a thread,
A hope that blooms where fears have tread.

So wear it close, this fragile grace,
Embrace the light, the love we chase.
For in this armor, hearts unite,
In joyous laughter, pure delight.

Enigmas Behind the Laughter

Laughter rings, a mystery spun,
In jests and giggles, hearts undone.
Yet deep within, an enigma glows,
A shadowed truth that seldom shows.

With every chuckle, layers peel,
The silent burdens we conceal.
What hides beneath the carefree sounds?
A kaleidoscope of thoughts that bounds.

In jest we hide our deepest fears,
A mask of joy that often tears.
The laughter echoes, light yet tough,
Yet still, our hearts can feel enough.

So listen close to laughter's song,
For in the light, the dark belongs.
An enigma wrapped in joy and cheer,
A testament that love is near.

The Philosophy of a Smile

What wisdom lies within a smile?
A spark of joy that travels miles.
In every curve, a tale is spun,
Connecting hearts, the soul's true run.

The philosophy of joy's design,
To bridge the gaps and intertwine.
With every gesture, bonds we weave,
A shared existence, we believe.

In silence speaks a language pure,
A gentle warmth, forever sure.
The world expands when smiles are shared,
A simple act, yet deeply cared.

So cultivate this precious art,
A smile can heal the aching heart.
For in its light, we find our place,
A dance of love, a warm embrace.

The Secrets Underneath the Cheer

In laughter's echo, shadows play,
Beneath the joy, where secrets lay.
A smile can hide a thousand fears,
The truth masked by the festive cheers.

Whispers of sorrow float in air,
Dancing like ghosts that linger there.
For every grin, a tale untold,
A heart encased in silence, bold.

Behind the sparkles, tears may flow,
Each heartbeat caught in hidden woe.
Yet still we wear the masks of bright,
The secrets hidden out of sight.

So let us share, just for a while,
The burdens held behind each smile.
For in the trust of honest hearts,
The secrets fade, and hope restarts.

Dance of Hidden Tears

In the quiet corners of the night,
Dancers twirl, their movements light.
Yet every spin hides well a tear,
A silent song of all their fear.

The music plays, a haunting tune,
Beneath the glow of a silver moon.
Each step they take, a story spun,
Of battles fought, and victories won.

With every glance, a look askew,
The dance reveals what none yet knew.
A fragile strength in each embrace,
In secret steps, they find their place.

But once the music fades away,
The hidden tears can no longer stay.
They spill like rain upon the floor,
The dance of hearts, forevermore.

Luminous Deception

Beneath the glow of starry skies,
Lies a world veiled in sweet disguise.
With every gleam, a truth unclear,
In luminous light, the dark draws near.

The shining paths lead hearts astray,
While shadows whisper, beg and play.
What glimmers bright may hide the pain,
In dazzling hues, a hint of rain.

The glow invites, but dusk is close,
Fleeting smiles hide the utmost woes.
In every shard of light, a cost,
For all that's found must first be lost.

Yet still we chase that radiant spark,
In dreams we wander, lost in the dark.
And if we find, in depths of night,
The truest glow is born from light.

The Smile Trade

In bustling streets, the traders stand,
Exchanging smiles, a gentle hand.
For joy's a coin, we give and take,
Yet underneath, the hearts may break.

Each grin a mask for deeper fears,
As laughter hides the quiet tears.
In every deal, a story's spun,
What's given freely is rarely won.

The currency of charming grace,
Conceals the wounds we can't erase.
Yet still we barter, day by day,
For fragile hopes in the smile trade.

But what if laughter told the truth?
A world laid bare, a quest for proof.
In every trade, let kindness reign,
For smiles shared can soothe the pain.

Whims of the Heart

In the garden of dreams, we play,
Chasing shadows that dance and sway.
Whispers of wishes float through the air,
A fleeting moment beyond compare.

Love's gentle breeze stirs the night,
Softly it cradles, feels so right.
With every flutter, hearts ignite,
A symphony in the pale moonlight.

Yet, the heart wanders, swift and bold,
In search of stories yet to be told.
Through laughter and tears, hopes intertwine,
Navigating paths made divine.

Oh, whims of the heart, wild and free,
A tapestry woven, you and me.
Each thread a memory, bright and clear,
Together forever, we shall persevere.

The Vessel of a Cheerful Heart

In the glow of the morning light,
A vessel brims with joy in sight.
Laughter bubbles and dances within,
Carrying warmth to all who begin.

With each smile, a spark ignites,
In the rhythm of days and starry nights.
The world unfolds in colors bright,
A tapestry woven in pure delight.

When clouds gather, and shadows loom,
This cheerful heart will chase the gloom.
With kindness wrapped in every beat,
Transforming sorrows to life's sweet treat.

In harmony's embrace, let's draw near,
A vessel brimming with love and cheer.
Together we sail through the stormy sea,
With a cheerful heart, forever free.

The Mirage of Happiness

Like a whisper on the breeze, it glides,
A mirage that hides, then softly collides.
In the realm of dreams where wishes roam,
Searching for peace, we find no home.

Each glimmer fades as sunlight breaks,
The chase for joy, a dance it makes.
Through hidden paths, we roam and stray,
In the mirage of happiness, we play.

Yet, what's real is the love we share,
In laughter's embrace, we find our dare.
With every heartbeat, the truth unfolds,
Happiness lies in moments bold.

So, hold fast to the moments bright,
Amidst the mirage, we find our light.
In every heartbeat, let love resound,
In the journey of life, pure joy is found.

Layers of Laughter

Beneath the surface, laughter spins,
In layers woven, friendship begins.
Each chuckle, a thread in a vibrant quilt,
A sanctuary of joy, carefully built.

From gentle giggles to hearty roars,
In each shared moment, our spirit soars.
Unraveling stories, silly and sweet,
Layers of laughter, a timeless treat.

In the trials of life, it's our cure,
A balm for the soul, comforting and pure.
With every layer, new memories form,
In laughter's embrace, we weather the storm.

So let us gather, in joy's embrace,
Peeling the layers, finding our place.
In laughter, we shine, bright and bold,
A treasure of moments, a joy to behold.

Navigating the Joyful Facade

Beneath the laughter lies a sigh,
With every cheer, a whispered why.
We dance along this masquerade,
In bright costumes, our truths are laid.

In sunlight's glow, we play our parts,
Hiding shadows in our hearts.
A fragile smile, a fleeting glance,
We twirl in hope, we long to dance.

But in the night, the masks may slip,
Revealing pain on a tender lip.
Yet still we forge, with joyful grace,
As if each moment's a warm embrace.

So let us weave this vibrant thread,
Despite the fears that go unsaid.
For in the joy, we find our way,
Navigating night to greet the day.

The Choreography of Smiles

In corridors of laughter bright,
We spin and sway in pure delight.
Each smile a note, a subtle cue,
A dance of souls, a bond anew.

With every twirl, a secret shared,
In every glance, a heart laid bare.
We leap through moments, light as air,
In rhythm's flow, we shed our care.

Yet underneath the graceful show,
Lie stories that we rarely show.
A choreography of sighs,
Where truth and artifice collide and rise.

Together we dance, a fleeting bliss,
In this grand ballet, we dare to risk.
For every smile, a world apart,
The choreography of the heart.

Radiant Facades of Deceit

In mirrors bright, we pose and preen,
Radiant facades, a glossy sheen.
Behind the glow, a restless mind,
A storm of thoughts we try to hide.

With painted masks, we craft our air,
An artful guise, a polished flare.
But whispers linger, shadows play,
As truth and pretense dance away.

In laughter shared, a brittle shell,
A fortress built, yet hard to dwell.
Each shining smile, a flickering light,
Guiding us through the veil of night.

Yet still we bask in this charade,
In radiant dreams we've often made.
For deep within, the truth lies bare,
Amid the radiant masks we wear.

Tapestry of Hidden Hearts

We weave our stories, thread by thread,
In colors bold, in whispers said.
A tapestry of hopes and fears,
Woven tightly through the years.

In every stitch, a secret sewn,
In silence kept, love has grown.
Each strand a journey, sometimes torn,
Yet through the fray, new dreams are born.

We touch the fabric, soft and strong,
In tangled fibers, we belong.
A hidden heart, a life entwined,
In this great work, our souls aligned.

So let us cherish, thread by thread,
The tapestries of all we've said.
For in the patterns, bright and stark,
We find our truth; we leave our mark.

The Jests We Keep

In laughter's cloak, we dance and play,
Hiding sorrows that fade away.
Each smile a cover, a clever guise,
Behind the mask, a heart that cries.

We jest and weave our tales so bright,
Yet shadows linger, out of sight.
For joy's a game we often feign,
A fragile heart bears all the pain.

In cheerful tones, we raise a cheer,
While silence screams what we don't hear.
The jokes we tell, a fleeting jest,
Disguise the truths that never rest.

So here's to laughter, sweet and pure,
A balm for wounds that need a cure.
Yet in the mirth, let's not forget,
The jests we keep, a heavy debt.

The Enigma of Joyful Exteriors

A facade bright, with colors bold,
Yet secrets lie, untold, and cold.
Smiles painted on, with perfect strokes,
Beneath the surface, silence chokes.

The joy we flaunt, a clever guise,
To hide the truth behind our eyes.
We wear our bliss like silken threads,
While inside, doubt and worry spreads.

What does it mean to show delight?
To hide the tears that steal the night?
Each laugh a mask, we deftly wear,
A struggle hidden, too great to bear.

In crowded rooms, we play our part,
Yet loneliness can fill the heart.
The enigma spins in vibrant hues,
What joy exists when we hide the blues?

Bright Faces, Burdened Souls

Bright faces shine in morning light,
But shadows linger just out of sight.
With laughter loud, and voices clear,
The burdens grow, yet none appear.

In every grin, a story hides,
Of sleepless nights and tempest tides.
A joyful laugh can mask a sigh,
While deep inside, the spirits cry.

We walk on streets with heads held high,
But inside hearts, we want to fly.
The weight we carry, forged in pain,
Is buried deep, like autumn rain.

So when you see a smiling face,
Remember, joy's a tight embrace.
For every bright, there's also dark,
And every soul, a silent spark.

The Elegy of a Grinning Mask

A grinning mask upon my face,
Hides the truth, my secret space.
With every laugh, a tear is thrown,
An elegy for the heart alone.

Each chuckle echoes, yet feels so fake,
A dance of shadows, hearts that ache.
We gather joy as if it's real,
A fragile mask, a pain conceal.

But in the night, the mask will break,
And in that moment, we will ache.
The elegy sings of love once lost,
Of laughter dulled, and bitter cost.

So seek the light within the gloom,
And let the weary heart find room.
For every mask that one must wear,
There's always hope, beyond despair.

Joy's Underbelly

Beneath the laughter, whispers low,
Shadows dance where feelings flow.
A smile masks the aching truth,
While joy conceals the tale of youth.

In sunlight's warmth, the darkness hides,
A fragile heart that bides and bides.
With each bright cheer, a faint dismay,
Joy's underbelly, softly sways.

Yet still the heart seeks out the light,
Amidst the dark, it cages fright.
A blended hue of hopes and fears,
Crafting solace from the tears.

Beneath the surface, life unfolds,
A tapestry of blues and golds.
In every joy, a hint of ache,
The bittersweet, a heart can make.

The Illusion of Delight

A radiant glow from faces bright,
But hidden depths veiled from the sight.
The laughter rings, a siren's call,
Promising joy, yet none at all.

Candy-coated dreams, a shell,
For deep inside, a hollow well.
Each grin a mask, a fragile guise,
Concealing sorrow in their eyes.

With every cheer, the truth grows thin,
While shadows creep, the doubts set in.
What seems so sweet can turn so sour,
An echo lost, loses its power.

Yet in that space, a flicker glows,
A flicker of what nobody knows.
The heart can mend with gentle light,
And find the way from dark to bright.

Revelations in the Gleeful Glint

In moments bright, the truth unfurls,
Gleaming glints in a world of pearls.
But joy can twist, a double edge,
Inviting woes to form a hedge.

A childlike laugh, pure and sincere,
Yet deep within, a trembling fear.
For every laugh, a shadow trails,
A gentle truth that quietly hails.

Moments clash, a stormy fight,
Where laughter hides the deepest fright.
The gleeful glint, a bright veneer,
Hiding tales we dread to hear.

But as eyes close and hearts embrace,
A bittersweet dance finds its place.
In joy, in pain, a thread we sew,
Revelations come where few will go.

Echoes of Hidden Sorrow

In every joy, a whispered sigh,
An echo soft, the heart's goodbye.
The laughter drowns, yet still it yearns,
For love that fades, for time that burns.

Amidst celebrations, shadows creep,
In joyful moments, secrets keep.
Behind the smiles, a distant trace,
Of sorrow's song, of lost embrace.

Like fleeting ghost, they float and swirl,
In laughter's grasp, their spirits twirl.
Each cheer a mask, a fleeting ruse,
Where hidden sorrow paints the views.

Yet still we dance, we love, we strive,
In echoes soft, the hopes alive.
For joy and pain, a woven thread,
In life's embrace, both loved and led.

Secrets in the Curve of Lips

Whispers linger, soft as air,
A smile that hides a tale so rare.
In shadows cast by fleeting light,
Secrets dance in the silence of night.

Glossy sheen, a fleeting glance,
Promises weave in a secret dance.
Each curve a story, silence sharp,
Lips conceal the beating heart.

Sips of laughter, shadows play,
In the garden where emotions sway.
A moment captured, time stands still,
In every smile, a hidden thrill.

Underneath a gaze so deep,
Lies a promise, a vow to keep.
Secrets in the curve of lips,
Life's sweetest taste in gentle sips.

The Silent Weep

Beneath the calm, where shadows creep,
Lies a sorrow, a silent weep.
Tears unshed, like stars secure,
In aching hearts, they long for cure.

Echoes linger, lost in time,
Murmurs dance to a haunting rhyme.
Every breath a whispered plea,
In twilight's hush, we cease to be.

Night descends with velvet grace,
In solitude's embrace, we trace.
Each heartbeat a reminder clear,
Of dreams once held, now lost in fear.

Yet in this dark, a flicker glows,
A spark of hope through all that flows.
The silent weep may softly fade,
To light the path where love is laid.

Bright Eyes

In the morning, where sunlight streams,
Bright eyes shimmer, igniting dreams.
A world awakens with each new glance,
In vibrant hues, life finds its dance.

Glistening pools of pure delight,
Reflecting warmth in the softest light.
With every blink, stories unfold,
Whispers of joy in shades of gold.

Eyes that sparkle, laughter's grace,
In every moment, a warm embrace.
They hold the wisdom of untold years,
A canvas painted with hopes and fears.

Bright eyes see the beauty rare,
In simple things, in love's sweet care.
They shine with passion, fierce and true,
In the heart's garden, ever new.

Lingering Shadows

Shadows stretch as the daylight wanes,
Whispers of dusk in ethereal chains.
Figures dance in the twilight's glow,
Lingering tales in the afterflow.

Each moment captured, fading fast,
Echoes of memories from the past.
Thoughts entwined in the evening's sigh,
Where shadows linger, as time slips by.

Secrets spoken in the softest shade,
Hints of laughter in silence laid.
Beneath the stars, we find our place,
In the lingering shadows, we embrace.

So hold on tight as the world turns slow,
In the hush of night, let love's warmth flow.
For shadows may linger, but love will light,
The path we tread in the coming night.

Radiance with a Hint of Gloom

In the dawn where colors blend,
Radiance shines, yet heart may bend.
Light cascades through broken seams,
With hints of gloom in fragile dreams.

Golden rays on the horizon spread,
Yet dark clouds float, where hope once led.
Joy intermingles with sorrow's song,
In this life where all belong.

Amidst the beauty, shadows play,
In every heart, a price to pay.
For every smile, a tear will flow,
Radiance thrives, but gloom may grow.

So we embrace the light and shade,
In this tapestry that we have made.
For in the balance, we find our way,
Radiance shines through the darkest day.

The Layers of Laughter

In whispers soft, joy leaps high,
Beneath the smiles, a subtle sigh.
Each chuckle hides, a story deep,
Of moments lost, in memories we keep.

A giggle glows, like morning light,
Yet shadows dance, just out of sight.
We wear our glee like a warm coat,
But hearts can wade in a different boat.

When laughter rings, it fills the air,
But silent tears, can linger there.
Underneath the vibrant cheer,
Are layers of doubts that reappear.

So cherish joy, but know the truth,
That laughter's depth holds shades of youth.
A smile may mask a fragile heart,
In every jest, there's a hidden part.

Chasing Shadows of Truth

In the quiet dusk, questions arise,
Where truth lies hidden, behind disguise.
We chase the whispers, swift and fleet,
In shadows dancing, lies the beat.

Under moonlight, doubts are cast,
Moments linger, echoes vast.
With every step, a choice to make,
In the pursuit of light, hearts may break.

Yet in the chase, a spark ignites,
Guiding souls through darkest nights.
Truth, like a river, flows and bends,
Leading us on, as the daylight ends.

So we pursue, both brave and bold,
In shadows, stories yet untold.
Each step we take, unveils the plan,
Chasing truth, hand in hand.

When Cheerfulness Fades

The sun dips low, the shadows grow,
Where laughter once danced, now silence flows.
Once vivid hues, now shades of grey,
As cheerfulness fades, we drift away.

A vacant smile, a distant gaze,
In the fading light, we lose our ways.
Memories linger, like soft-spun threads,
While echoes whisper of words unsaid.

Days stretch long, like shadows cast,
In silent rooms, we tell the past.
The warmth departs, like evening's close,
When cheerfulness fades, sorrow grows.

Yet through the dark, a flicker remains,
Hope finds a way through life's refrains.
In every heart, a spark can ignite,
A dawn can rise from the velvet night.

Behind the Bright Lights

In the glimmering glow of the stage,
Stars shine bright, yet hide their age.
Behind the curtain, shadows play,
Mysteries linger, just out of sway.

Each spotlight beams, a dazzling show,
While hearts may tremble, beneath the glow.
The world outside may not perceive,
The weight of dreams we dare to weave.

As laughter echoes, applause takes flight,
Yet still we battle, against the night.
With every act, a truth laid bare,
Behind the bright lights, lives in despair.

But in the dusk, resilience springs,
In whispered hopes, the silent sings.
For every soul, a story waits,
Behind the scenes, where hope creates.

Beneath the Bright Horizon

The sun will rise on fields of gold,
Where dreams are rich and stories told.
A breeze will dance with gentle grace,
Painting smiles on every face.

We wander far, yet find our way,
Through shadows cast by yesterday.
With every step, new hopes ignite,
Beneath the bright horizon's light.

The clouds may gather, dark and dense,
But hearts will sing in strong suspense.
For every storm must fade and part,
To let the sun embrace the heart.

Together here, our spirits soar,
With love that blooms on every shore.
Beneath the sky, we stand as one,
Our journey bright, our battles won.

The Weight of a Laughing Heart

In laughter lies a vivid spark,
That lights the shadows, leaves a mark.
A gentle tug, a joyful pull,
That fills the air, both light and full.

When burdens wear the soul down slow,
A chuckle breaks the heavy flow.
With every giggle, moments shared,
The weight of sorrow is impaired.

Together we can face the dark,
With mirth we carry, joy we spark.
In whispered jokes and stories bright,
We find our way to pure delight.

The weight of grief begins to lift,
Replaced by love, our precious gift.
So let us revel, sing, and sway,
Embracing life in a dance of play.

Mirth Wrapped in Mystery

In twilight's glow, the whispers weave,
A tale of joy that love can leave.
With secrets spun from silver threads,
A tapestry where laughter spreads.

Beneath the stars, we sit and smile,
As mysteries unfold awhile.
With every glance, a spark ignites,
In shadows deep, our hearts take flight.

The world may hide, obscured from sight,
But laughter breaks the veil of night.
In simple things, the truth we find,
A bond of hearts, forever twined.

So let us roam where secrets dwell,
In mirth and joy, we cast our spell.
Embracing life's enchanting game,
Wrapped in mystery, love remains.

Smiling Through the Storm

The tempest roars, the winds do howl,
But in our hearts, we're steadfast, prowl.
With laughter bright as lightning strikes,
We find our strength in joy's delights.

Through rain-soaked days and endless night,
We hold our heads, we shine our light.
For every drop that falls like tears,
We dance and twirl, dismissing fears.

We grasp the hands that reach for ours,
Together, we will count the stars.
In chaos, let our spirits sing,
A melody that hope will bring.

So let the storm swirl wildly 'round,
We'll wear our smiles, be joy profound.
Through every trial, we shall see,
A brighter world, both wild and free.